From Fear to Freedom

A Guide to Escaping Coercive Control

HOPE, HEALING AND RISING STRONG

M L Runcsnk

FROM FEAR TO FREEDOM: A GUIDE TO ESCAPING COERCIVE CONTROL

Trient Press
3375 S Rainbow Blvd
#81710, SMB 13135
Las Vegas,NV 89180

Ordering Information:
Quantity sales. Special discounts are available on quantity purchases by corporations, associations, and others. For details, contact the publisher at the address above.
Orders by U.S. trade bookstores and wholesalers. Please contact Trient Press: Tel: (775) 996-3844; or visit www.trientpress.com.

Printed in the United States of America

Publisher's Cataloging-in-Publication data
Ruscsak, M.L.
A title of a book :From Fear to Freedom: A Guide to Escaping Coercive Control
ISBN

Paper Back   979-8-88990-063-4
Ebook   979-8-88990-064-1

Chapter 1 Introduction

Chapter 2 Understanding Coercive Control

Chapter 3 Recognizing Coercive Control

Chapter 4 Escaping Coercive Control

Chapter 5 Healing from Coercive Control

Chapter 6 Rising Strong After Coercive Control

Chapter 7 Conclusion

Dear Reader,

Thanks for picking up my book, "From Fear to Freedom: A Guide to Escaping Coercive Control." I'm so excited to share this journey with you as we explore the dynamics of coercive control and work towards healing and finding a path towards freedom.

In this book, we're going to dive deep into what coercive control is, how it works, and the impact it has on victims. We'll explore the many tactics used by abusers, such as emotional abuse, isolation, intimidation, financial control, and physical violence. We'll also hear from survivors who have escaped coercive control and learn from their experiences.

One of the things that makes this book unique is the inclusion of survivor stories. These stories are incredibly powerful and serve as a reminder that you're not alone in your experiences. By hearing from others who have been through similar situations, you may find inspiration and hope for your own journey.

Another important aspect of this book is the use of journal exercises. These exercises will help you to reflect on your own experiences and emotions, and work towards understanding and healing from the trauma of coercive control. I truly believe that writing down your thoughts and feelings can be a powerful tool for healing, and I'm excited to share this practice with you.

Throughout the book, we'll also discuss the importance of seeking support from trained professionals and creating a safety plan if you're currently experiencing coercive control. We'll explore ways that society as a whole can work towards preventing coercive control, such as creating laws and policies that protect victims and promoting healthy relationships built on mutual respect and equality.

In conclusion, this book is all about understanding and healing from the trauma of coercive control. By exploring the dynamics of this form of abuse and hearing from survivors who have escaped it, you'll gain a deeper understanding of your own experiences and find hope for your own journey towards freedom. So let's dive in and get started!

CHAPTER 1 INTRODUCTION

❖ Definition of coercive control
❖ Importance of understanding coercive control

Welcome to "From Fear to Freedom: A Guide to Escaping Coercive Control." This book is the final installment in my self-help series, Hope, Healing, and Rising Strong. Coercive control is a pervasive and insidious form of domestic violence that affects millions of people worldwide. This book is for those who are currently experiencing coercive control, those who have escaped it, and those who want to learn more about this issue.

Throughout the pages of this book, you will find survivor stories from people who have experienced coercive control firsthand. These stories are powerful and will give you a glimpse into the reality of living with this form of abuse. The survivors' stories are intended to inspire and provide hope to those who may feel trapped or hopeless. You are not alone, and there is a way out.

In addition to the survivor stories, this book includes journal exercises. These exercises are designed to help you reflect on your experiences, process your emotions, and develop strategies for healing and moving forward. The journal exercises are optional, but I encourage you to use them as a tool for self-discovery and growth.

The goal of this book is to provide a comprehensive guide for understanding and escaping coercive control. It is my hope that this book will be a valuable resource for anyone who wants to learn more about this issue and how to overcome it. Whether you are a survivor, a friend or family member of someone who is experiencing coercive control, or a professional working in the field of domestic violence, this book is for you.

Thank you for choosing to read this book. I hope that it will provide you with the knowledge, tools, and inspiration you need to escape coercive control and live a life of freedom and fulfillment.

Definition of coercive control

Coercive control is a pattern of behavior that an abuser uses to gain power and control over their victim. It is a form of domestic violence that often goes unrecognized because it is not always physical. Instead, the abuser uses emotional, psychological, and financial tactics to manipulate and control the victim. Understanding the dynamics of coercive control is crucial in identifying and addressing this form of abuse.

Definition and Explanation of Coercive Control

Coercive control is a form of domestic violence that involves ongoing and systematic abuse aimed at controlling the victim's behavior and limiting their freedom. It is a pattern of behavior that is used to gain power and control over the victim, and it is often used in intimate partner relationships. Coercive control is not always physical, but it can be just as damaging as physical violence.

Coercive control is characterized by the abuser's use of a variety of tactics to control the victim, including emotional abuse, financial abuse, isolation, and intimidation. The abuser may use tactics such as gaslighting, verbal abuse, threats, and manipulation to gain control over the victim. The goal of coercive control is to create an environment in which the victim is entirely dependent on the abuser and has no power or control over their own life.

Types of Coercive Control

Coercive control can take many different forms, and the tactics used by the abuser can vary widely. Some of the most common types of coercive control include:

Emotional abuse - The abuser may use emotional abuse to manipulate and control the victim, using tactics such as gaslighting, belittling, and humiliating the victim.

Financial abuse - The abuser may control the victim's finances, limiting their access to money or refusing to allow them to work.

Isolation - The abuser may isolate the victim from friends and family, making it difficult for the victim to leave the relationship.

Intimidation - The abuser may use threats or intimidation to control the victim, such as threatening to harm them or their loved ones.

Dynamics of Coercive Control Relationships

The dynamics of coercive control relationships are complex and often difficult to understand. In a coercive control relationship, the abuser is always seeking to gain power and control over the victim. They may use a variety of tactics to achieve this, including emotional abuse, financial control, and isolation.

The victim in a coercive control relationship may feel trapped and powerless. They may believe that they have no way out of the relationship and no ability to make decisions for themselves. The victim may also feel ashamed or embarrassed to admit that they are being abused, which can make it challenging to seek help.

Effects of Coercive Control on the Victim

The effects of coercive control on the victim can be severe and long-lasting. Victims of coercive control may experience a range of physical and emotional effects, including:

Anxiety and depression - The victim may feel anxious or depressed as a result of the ongoing abuse and manipulation.

Low self-esteem - The victim may begin to doubt their own abilities and feel worthless as a result of the abuse.

Post-traumatic stress disorder (PTSD) - The victim may develop PTSD as a result of the ongoing abuse and trauma.

Physical symptoms - The victim may experience physical symptoms such as headaches, stomach problems, and fatigue as a result of the stress and anxiety caused by the abuse.

In Conclusion

Understanding the dynamics of coercive control is crucial in identifying and addressing this form of abuse. Coercive control is a pattern of behavior that an abuser uses to gain power and control over their victim. It is not always easy to recognize coercive control, as it can be subtle and insidious, but it is important to be aware of the signs and to take action to address the abuse.

One way to address coercive control is to seek support from trained professionals who can help victims identify the abuse and develop a safety plan. This may involve reaching out to domestic violence hotlines, seeking counseling or therapy, or working with an advocate to develop a plan to leave the relationship safely.

It is also important for society as a whole to recognize the prevalence of coercive control and work towards preventing it. This can include educating the public about the signs of abuse, creating laws and policies that protect victims, and promoting healthy relationships built on mutual respect and equality.

In this book, we will explore the many aspects of coercive control, from the tactics used by abusers to the impact it has on victims. We will also hear from survivors who have escaped coercive control and learn from their experiences. Through journal exercises and reflection, we will work towards understanding and healing from the trauma of coercive control and finding a path towards freedom.

It is my hope that this book will serve as a guide for anyone who has experienced coercive control, helping them to understand their experiences and find a way forward towards a life free from abuse.

Importance of understanding coercive control

Coercive control is a form of abuse that is often misunderstood and overlooked. Victims of coercive control may not even realize that they are being abused, as the tactics used by abusers can be subtle and insidious. In order to address and prevent coercive control, it is crucial to understand what it is and how it works.

What is Coercive Control?

Coercive control is a pattern of behavior that an abuser uses to gain power and control over their victim. It can involve a wide range of tactics, including emotional abuse, isolation, intimidation, financial control, and physical violence. Coercive control is not a single act of violence or abuse, but rather a sustained campaign of abuse that can last for years.

One of the key aspects of coercive control is that the abuser uses tactics that may not be illegal on their own, but when used in combination, create a situation of ongoing abuse and control. For example, an abuser may use verbal put-downs, limit their partner's access to money and transportation, and control their movements to keep them isolated from friends and family.

Why is Understanding Coercive Control Important?

Understanding coercive control is important for a number of reasons. First and foremost, it can help victims to recognize that they are being abused and seek help. Coercive control can be difficult to identify, especially if the victim has been isolated from friends and family or made to feel that the abuse is their fault. By understanding what coercive control is and how it works, victims can begin to recognize the signs of abuse and take steps to protect themselves.

Secondly, understanding coercive control is important for society as a whole. Coercive control is a widespread problem that affects people of all genders, races, and socioeconomic backgrounds. By understanding the dynamics of coercive control, we can work towards preventing it from happening in the first place. This may involve creating laws and policies that protect victims, providing education and resources to the public, and promoting healthy relationships built on mutual respect and equality.

Lastly, understanding coercive control is important for the healing and recovery of survivors. Victims of coercive control may experience a range of emotions, including fear, shame, guilt, and isolation. By understanding that they are not alone in their experiences, survivors can begin to heal and recover from the trauma of abuse.

Conclusion

In order to address and prevent coercive control, it is crucial to understand what it is and how it works. Coercive control is a pattern of behavior used by abusers to gain power and control over their victim, and can involve a range of tactics. By understanding coercive control, victims can recognize the signs of abuse and seek help, society can work towards preventing it from happening in the first place, and survivors can begin to heal and recover from the trauma of abuse.

Journal Exercises

Reflect on Your Understanding of Coercive Control: Take a few minutes to write down what you understand about coercive control. How do you define it?

_____

_____

_____

_____

_____

_____

_____

_____

_____

_____

_____

What are some of the tactics used by abusers? This exercise can help you identify any gaps in your knowledge and set the foundation for further exploration in the book.

_____

_____

_____

_____

_____

_____

_____

_____

_____

_____

_____

_____

_____

Explore Your Emotions:
Write down how you feel about your experiences with coercive control. Are you angry, sad, scared, or all of the above?

_____

_____

_____

_____

_____

_____

_____

_____

_____

How have these emotions impacted your life? This exercise can help you to better understand and process your feelings.

_____

_____

_____

_____

_____

_____

_____

_____

_____

_____

_____

_____

Identify Patterns of Control:

Think back on your experiences with coercive control and write down any patterns of behavior you noticed. For example, did the abuser try to isolate you from friends and family?

_____

_____

_____

_____

_____

_____

_____

_____

_____

Did they use financial control as a way to manipulate you? This exercise can help you recognize the tactics used by your abuser and give you a starting point for healing.

_____

_____

_____

_____

_____

_____

_____

_____

_____

_____

_____

_____

_____

Reflect on Your Support System:
Write down the people in your life who have been supportive of you during your experiences with coercive control. How have they helped you?

_____

_____

_____

_____

_____

_____

_____

_____

_____

_____

How have they made you feel? This exercise can help you identify the people you can turn to for support during difficult times.

_____

_____

_____

_____

_____

_____

_____

_____

_____

_____

_____

_____

Set Goals for Your Healing:
Take some time to write down your goals for healing from the trauma of coercive control. What do you hope to achieve?

_____

_____

_____

_____

_____

_____

_____

_____

_____

_____

_____

_____

What steps can you take to get there? This exercise can help you stay focused on your healing journey and give you a sense of purpose and direction.

_____

_____

_____

_____

_____

_____

_____

_____

_____

_____

_____

CHAPTER 2 UNDERSTANDING COERCIVE CONTROL

- ❖ Definition and explanation of coercive control
- ❖ Types of coercive control
- ❖ Dynamics of coercive control relationships
- ❖ Effects of coercive control on the victim

Hey there, it's M.L.Ruscsak here, and in this chapter, we're going to dive deep into the topic of coercive control. If you're reading this book, chances are you've experienced coercive control in some form or another, and it's important to understand what this type of abuse looks like and how it works.

So, what is coercive control? Simply put, it's a pattern of behavior that an abuser uses to gain power and control over their victim. This can take many forms, from emotional abuse to financial control, and even physical violence. The abuser may use a variety of tactics to exert control, such as isolating their victim from friends and family, controlling their finances, and manipulating their emotions.

It's important to note that coercive control is not just about physical violence. In fact, many victims of coercive control may not experience physical violence at all. Instead, the abuse can be more subtle and insidious, taking the form of manipulation, intimidation, and emotional abuse. For more detail on each kind of abuse please see the rest of the "Hope, Healing and Rising Strong" series.

In this chapter, we'll explore the different types of coercive control, from emotional abuse to financial control, and discuss how each type of abuse works. We'll also look at the dynamics of coercive control relationships, and how the abuser uses tactics such as gaslighting and blame-shifting to maintain control over their victim.

It's also important to understand the effects that coercive control can have on the victim. Victims of coercive control may experience a range of emotions, from fear and anxiety to depression and hopelessness. The abuse can also have long-term effects on the victim's mental and physical health, as well as their ability to form healthy relationships in the future.

In conclusion, understanding the dynamics of coercive control is crucial in identifying and addressing this form of abuse. By exploring the different types of coercive control, the dynamics of abusive relationships, and the effects that the abuse can have on the victim, we can work towards creating a world where coercive control is not tolerated. So let's dive in and learn more about this important topic.

Definition and explanation of coercive control

Coercive control is a pattern of behavior that an abuser uses to gain power and control over their victim. This type of abuse is often more subtle than physical violence, but can be just as damaging. Coercive control can take many forms, including emotional abuse, financial control, and physical violence.

At the heart of coercive control is the abuser's desire to exert power and control over their victim. They may use a variety of tactics to achieve this, such as:

Isolating their victim from friends and family
Controlling their finances, including limiting their access to money or forcing them to account for every penny spent
Using emotional abuse, such as gaslighting or blame-shifting, to manipulate their victim's emotions and make them doubt themselves
Using physical violence or the threat of violence to maintain control

Coercive control can be incredibly difficult to recognize, both for the victim and for those around them. The abuser may appear charming and charismatic to outsiders, while the victim may feel trapped and helpless.

It's important to note that coercive control is not just about physical violence. While physical violence is certainly a form of coercive control, there are many other tactics that abusers may use to maintain control over their victims. Emotional abuse, financial control, and other forms of manipulation can be just as damaging and can leave long-lasting scars.

In order to recognize and address coercive control, it's important to understand the different types of abuse that can be used. By recognizing the tactics used by abusers and understanding the dynamics of abusive relationships, we can begin to take steps towards creating a world where coercive control is not tolerated.

In the next chapter, we'll explore the different types of coercive control in more detail, and discuss how each type of abuse works. So stay tuned, and let's continue our journey towards understanding and addressing this important issue.

Types of Coercive Control - A Survivor's Perspective

Hey there, I'm a survivor of coercive control, and I'm here to share my story with you. It's not an easy story to tell, but I hope that by sharing my experiences, I can help others recognize the signs of coercive control and find the strength to break free.

In this chapter, we'll be exploring the different types of coercive control that my abuser used, and how they affected me.

First up, there's emotional abuse. This type of control can be incredibly subtle, but it can have a devastating impact on the victim. My abuser would constantly make me doubt myself and my own perceptions of reality, telling me that I was crazy and that I was the problem in our relationship. It was a slow and insidious process, but it left me feeling powerless and trapped.

Another tactic that my abuser used was financial control. They would limit my access to money, and would use money as a way to manipulate me. For example, they would threaten to cut off financial support if I didn't do what they wanted. It was a form of control that left me feeling completely dependent on my abuser, unable to leave the relationship because I didn't have the financial resources to support myself.

Unfortunately, my abuser didn't stop at emotional and financial control. They also resorted to physical violence, hitting and pushing me, and threatening me with harm if I didn't comply with their demands. This type of control was terrifying, but it was also the form of abuse that was easiest for others to recognize.

Sexual coercion was another form of control that my abuser used. They would pressure me into engaging in sexual acts that I wasn't comfortable with, or would use sex as a way to manipulate me. This type of abuse can be incredibly difficult to come to terms with, as there is often a lot of shame and stigma associated with it.

Lastly, my abuser used isolation as a way to maintain control over me. They would try to limit my contact with friends and family, and would discourage me from pursuing my own interests or hobbies. This left me feeling completely alone and helpless, and made it even harder for me to break free from the cycle of abuse.

In conclusion, the different types of coercive control can be incredibly damaging, and can leave the victim feeling trapped and powerless. If you or someone you know is experiencing coercive control, please know that there is help available. It's never too late to seek support and break free from the cycle of abuse. Remember, you deserve to be treated with respect and dignity, and there are people out there who can help you on your journey to healing.

Journal Exercises

Reflect on your past relationships and identify any instances of emotional abuse that you may have experienced. How did these experiences make you feel? Did they impact your self-esteem or sense of self-worth?

_____

_____

_____

_____

_____

_____

_____

_____

_____

_____

_____

What steps can you take to heal from these experiences?

_____

_____

_____

_____

_____

_____

_____

_____

_____

_____

_____

_____

_____

Think about a time when you felt financially dependent on someone else. How did this impact your relationship?

_____

_____

_____

_____

_____

_____

_____

_____

_____

Did it make you feel powerless or trapped?

_____

_____

_____

_____

_____

_____

_____

_____

_____

_____

_____

_____

How can you work towards financial independence and security in the future?

_____

_____

_____

_____

_____

_____

_____

_____

_____

_____

Consider a time when you witnessed or experienced physical violence in a relationship. How did you react in the moment?

_____

_____

_____

_____

_____

Did you seek help or support afterwards?

What can you do to support others who may be experiencing violence in their relationships?

_____

_____

_____

_____

_____

_____

_____

Reflect on a time when you felt pressure to engage in sexual activities that you weren't comfortable with. How did you respond in the moment?

_____

_____

_____

_____

_____

_____

_____

_____

_____

_____

Did you feel like you had agency and control over your own body?

_____

_____

_____

_____

_____

_____

_____

_____

_____

_____

_____

_____

How can you work towards building a healthier relationship with your sexuality and sexual boundaries?

_____

_____

_____

_____

_____

_____

_____

_____

_____

_____

Think about a time when you felt isolated or cut off from your friends and family. How did this impact your mental health and well-being?

_____

_____

_____

_____

_____

_____

_____

_____

_____

_____

_____

_____

Did you feel like you had the support and resources you needed to leave the situation?

_____

_____

_____

_____

_____

_____

_____

_____

_____

How can you build a support network and cultivate meaningful connections in your life?

_____

_____

_____

_____

_____

_____

_____

_____

_____

_____

_____

Consider the ways in which you may be perpetuating coercive control in your own relationships, whether consciously or unconsciously. How can you work towards recognizing and changing these patterns of behavior?

_____

_____

_____

_____

_____

_____

_____

_____

_____

_____

What steps can you take to foster healthier, more equitable relationships in your life?

_____

_____

_____
_____
_____
_____
_____
_____
_____
_____
_____
_____
_____

"The greatest glory in living lies not in never falling, but in rising every time we fall." - Nelson Mandela

Dynamics of coercive control relationships

Coercive control is a pattern of behavior that seeks to dominate and control another person, often through tactics such as isolation, manipulation, intimidation, and abuse. This pattern of behavior is often seen in relationships where one person is seeking to exert power and control over the other, and it can have devastating effects on the survivor's mental, emotional, and physical well-being. Understanding the dynamics of coercive control relationships can be crucial for survivors who are seeking to heal and move forward.

The Power Imbalance

At the core of a coercive control relationship is a power imbalance, where one person seeks to have complete control over the other. This power imbalance can take many forms, such as financial control, emotional manipulation, physical intimidation, or sexual coercion. In many cases, the abuser will use a combination of tactics to maintain their power and control over the survivor.

Isolation and Intimidation

One of the most common tactics used by abusers is isolation. This involves limiting the survivor's access to friends, family, and other sources of support. The abuser may also use intimidation tactics to control the survivor, such as threatening violence or making them feel like they are always being watched. This can make the survivor feel trapped and alone, with no one to turn to for help.

Gaslighting and Manipulation

Another common tactic used by abusers is gaslighting and manipulation. This involves distorting the survivor's sense of reality, making them doubt their own perceptions and experiences. The abuser may tell the survivor that they are overreacting, being too sensitive, or even imagining things. This can make the survivor feel like they are going crazy, and can make it difficult for them to trust their own thoughts and feelings.

Breaking Down Self-Worth

Abusers often seek to break down the survivor's sense of self-worth and self-esteem. They may criticize, belittle, or insult the survivor, or use other tactics to make them feel inferior or unworthy. This can be especially damaging for survivors who may already be struggling with low self-esteem or self-worth.

Reclaiming Power and Control

Despite the devastating effects of coercive control, survivors can reclaim their power and control over their own lives. This process may involve seeking support from friends, family, or a therapist, as well as developing coping strategies and self-care practices. It can also involve setting boundaries and establishing clear expectations for future relationships.

Healing and Moving Forward

Healing from the trauma of a coercive control relationship can take time, and may involve seeking professional support. Survivors may need to work through feelings of shame, guilt, and anger, and may need to relearn how to trust themselves and others. However, with support and guidance, survivors can rebuild their sense of self-worth and self-esteem, and move forward into a healthier and happier future.

Conclusion

Coercive control relationships are complex and often difficult to recognize. However, by understanding the dynamics of these relationships, survivors can begin to reclaim their power and control, and move forward into a brighter future. It's important to remember that healing is a process, and that there is no right or wrong way to go about it. The most important thing is to seek support, establish healthy boundaries, and prioritize self-care and self-compassion.

Effects of coercive control on the victim

Coercive control is a pattern of behavior used by abusers to maintain power and control over their partners. Victims of coercive control experience a wide range of negative effects that can last long after the relationship ends. In this chapter, we will explore some of the effects of coercive control on the victim.

Emotional Effects

One of the most common effects of coercive control on the victim is emotional trauma. Victims may experience feelings of fear, anxiety, depression, and helplessness. They may feel as if they are walking on eggshells around their abuser, afraid of setting them off. Over time, victims may begin to feel like they have lost their sense of self, as the abuser systematically undermines their confidence and self-worth.

Physical Effects

Coercive control can also have physical effects on the victim. Victims may experience headaches, stomachaches, and other physical symptoms of stress. They may also experience sleep disturbances and exhaustion from the constant stress of living in an abusive relationship. In some cases, victims may also experience physical violence, which can result in serious injuries.

Cognitive Effects

Victims of coercive control may also experience cognitive effects, such as difficulty concentrating, memory problems, and difficulty making decisions. This may be a result of the constant stress of living in an abusive relationship, as well as the abuser's efforts to control the victim's thoughts and actions.

Financial Effects

Abusers often use financial control as a tool to maintain power and control over their victims. Victims may be prevented from working or accessing financial resources, leaving them financially dependent on their abuser. This can make it difficult for victims to leave the relationship or rebuild their lives after leaving.

Social Effects

Coercive control can also have social effects on the victim. Abusers often isolate their victims from friends and family, leaving them with little support outside of the abusive relationship. Victims may also feel ashamed or embarrassed about their situation, which can make it difficult to reach out for help.

Effects on Children

Children who grow up in households where there is coercive control may also experience negative effects. They may witness violence or emotional abuse, which can lead to anxiety, depression, and other emotional problems. Children may also learn unhealthy relationship patterns, which can affect their own future relationships.

Recovering from the Effects of Coercive Control

Recovering from the effects of coercive control can be a long and difficult process. However, it is possible to heal and move forward with the right support and resources. If you are a victim of coercive control, it is important to reach out for help.

Counseling can be a powerful tool for healing from the emotional trauma of coercive control. A trained therapist can help you process your feelings and develop coping strategies to manage the effects of the abuse.

Support groups can also be helpful for victims of coercive control. These groups provide a safe space for victims to share their experiences and connect with others who have been through similar situations.

Financial resources, such as housing assistance and job training programs, can also be essential for victims who are trying to rebuild their lives after leaving an abusive relationship.

Ultimately, healing from the effects of coercive control requires a combination of emotional, social, and practical support. By seeking out the resources you need and surrounding yourself with a supportive network of friends and family, you can recover from the trauma of coercive control and create a healthy, fulfilling future for yourself.

In conclusion, the effects of coercive control on the victim can be far-reaching and long-lasting. However, with the right support

Journal exercices

Reflect on a time when you felt controlled or manipulated by someone else. How did it make you feel?

_____

_____

_____

_____

_____

_____

_____

_____

_____

_____

_____

Did it affect your sense of self-worth or self-esteem?

_____

_____

_____

_____

_____

_____

_____

_____

_____

_____

_____

_____

What boundaries did you feel were crossed, and how did it impact your trust in others?

_____

_____

_____

_____

_____

_____

_____

_____

_____

_____

_____

Write about a positive experience where you were able to set a boundary with someone who was trying to control you. How did it feel to assert yourself and prioritize your needs?

_____

_____

_____

_____

_____

_____

_____

_____

_____

_____

_____

_____

What did you learn from the experience, and how can you apply that to future situations where someone tries to control you?

_____

_____

_____

_____

_____

_____

_____

_____

_____

_____

Think about your support system and how they can help you recognize and respond to coercive control. Write about the people in your life who make you feel safe and supported. How can you reach out to them for help when you are feeling overwhelmed or controlled by someone else?

_____

_____

_____

_____

_____

_____

_____

_____

_____

_____

_____

Consider the different coping strategies you use to deal with the effects of coercive control. Write about the ones that have been most helpful for you, and think about other strategies you might try in the future. How can you make self-care and self-compassion a priority in your life?

Reflect on the ways in which coercive control has impacted your relationships with others. How has it affected your ability to trust others or feel safe in relationships? What steps can you take to rebuild your trust and create healthy boundaries with others? How can you communicate your needs and expectations clearly and assertively?

CHAPTER 3 RECOGNIZING COERCIVE CONTROL

❖ Signs and symptoms of coercive control
❖ The difference between healthy and unhealthy relationships
❖ Red flags in a relationship

In order to recognize and address coercive control in relationships, it's important to understand the difference between healthy and unhealthy dynamics. In this chapter, we'll explore the signs and symptoms of coercive control, as well as the red flags that may indicate an unhealthy relationship.

By identifying these warning signs, we can begin to take steps to protect ourselves and our loved ones from the damaging effects of coercive control. Remember, no one deserves to be treated with disrespect or to live in fear, and it's never too late to seek help and to break free from the cycle of abuse.

Signs and symptoms of coercive control

Hello, my name is Kym, and I'm a survivor of coercive control. In this chapter, we're going to take a closer look at the signs and symptoms of coercive control, and how to recognize when a relationship is unhealthy.

The Difference Between Healthy and Unhealthy Relationships
Before we dive into the signs of coercive control, it's important to understand the difference between healthy and unhealthy relationships. A healthy relationship is based on mutual respect, trust, and open communication. Each partner is allowed to have their own interests, friends, and hobbies, and they support each other in their pursuits.

On the other hand, an unhealthy relationship is characterized by one partner exerting power and control over the other. This can take many forms, including emotional abuse, physical violence, and coercion. In a healthy relationship, both partners feel valued and respected, while in an unhealthy relationship, one partner feels trapped and helpless.

Red Flags in a Relationship

When I first started dating my abuser, there were several red flags that I ignored. Looking back now, I can see how they were warning signs of the coercive control that was to come.

One of the first red flags was their possessiveness. They would get jealous if I spent time with friends or family, and would insist on knowing my every move. I thought it was just because they cared about me, but in reality, it was a way to control me.

Another red flag was their need for control. They would make all the decisions in our relationship, from where we went to eat to what I wore. I thought it was just because they had strong opinions, but again, it was a way to exert power over me.

As our relationship progressed, the red flags became more pronounced. They would belittle me, call me names, and tell me that I was worthless. They would threaten me with violence if I didn't comply with their demands. I felt trapped and alone, and I didn't know how to get out of the situation.

Recognizing Coercive Control

Coercive control is a pattern of behavior that an abuser uses to gain power and control over their victim. It can take many forms, including emotional abuse, financial control, physical violence, sexual coercion, and isolation.

One of the main signs of coercive control is a lack of freedom and independence. The victim may feel like they have to constantly justify their actions or ask for permission to do things. They may also be isolated from friends and family, and their abuser may try to control their finances or restrict their access to resources.

Another sign of coercive control is a lack of respect and empathy. The abuser may belittle the victim, call them names, or make them feel worthless. They may also disregard the victim's feelings and needs, and only focus on their own desires.

It's important to recognize that coercive control is a form of abuse, and it can be just as damaging as physical violence. If you or someone you know is experiencing coercive control, it's important to seek help and support. There are many resources available, including therapy, support groups, and hotlines.

In conclusion, recognizing the signs and symptoms of coercive control is crucial in identifying and addressing this form of abuse. As a survivor, it took me a long time to recognize what was happening to me and to seek help, but I'm grateful that I did. Remember, you deserve to be treated with respect and dignity, and there is help available if you need it.

"You deserve to be in a relationship where you are valued and respected, not controlled and belittled."

Reflect on past relationships or friendships that may have exhibited some red flags of coercive control. Write down specific examples of behaviors that made you uncomfortable or worried about your safety.

Think about the people in your life currently, including romantic partners, friends, and family members. Evaluate each relationship and ask yourself if there are any signs of coercive control. Write down any concerns or red flags you may have noticed.

Take time to consider what healthy relationships look like. Write down a list of traits that you value in relationships, such as respect, communication, and trust. Compare these traits to the behaviors that may indicate coercive control.

Write a letter to yourself, giving yourself permission to set boundaries and prioritize your own safety and well-being in all relationships. Share specific actions you can take to protect yourself, such as leaving a toxic relationship or seeking support from a trusted friend or therapist.

Create a safety plan for yourself in case of an emergency. Write down important phone numbers, the location of your important documents, and any resources that may be helpful in an abusive situation.

Consider seeking support from a therapist or support group. Write down any concerns or questions you may have about getting help, and make a plan for taking the first step towards seeking support.

"You are not alone, and you are not weak for seeking help. Your safety and well-being are important, and there are people and resources available to support you."

The difference between healthy and unhealthy relationships

When I reflect back on my past relationships, it's clear to me now that many of them were unhealthy. At the time, I didn't realize it, and I continued to engage in behaviors that were not good for my mental or emotional wellbeing. It wasn't until I learned about healthy relationships that I was able to recognize the signs of an unhealthy one.

In this chapter, we'll explore the differences between healthy and unhealthy relationships, and I'll share some of the warning signs that you may be in an unhealthy relationship.

What is a Healthy Relationship?

A healthy relationship is one that is built on mutual respect, trust, communication, and support. Both partners are able to express themselves openly and honestly, and they work together to find solutions to problems that arise. They each have their own interests and hobbies, but they also make time to spend together and engage in shared activities.

In a healthy relationship, both partners feel valued and appreciated for who they are, and they are able to maintain a sense of independence while still being committed to the relationship. Both partners are free to be themselves and to pursue their own goals, and they support each other in those endeavors.

What is an Unhealthy Relationship?

On the other hand, an unhealthy relationship is one in which one partner seeks to control or dominate the other. This can take many forms, including emotional abuse, physical violence, financial control, and sexual coercion.

In an unhealthy relationship, one partner may use manipulation, guilt, or fear to maintain control over the other. They may try to isolate their partner from friends and family, or they may try to limit their partner's access to money or resources.

Warning Signs of an Unhealthy Relationship

If you're not sure whether you're in a healthy or unhealthy relationship, here are some warning signs to look out for:

❖   Your partner is always putting you down or making you feel bad about yourself.

❖   Your partner is overly jealous or possessive.

❖   Your partner tries to control who you talk to or spend time with.

❖   Your partner threatens you or tries to intimidate you.

❖   Your partner pressures you into doing things that you're not comfortable with.

❖   Your partner withholds affection or attention as a way to punish you.

❖   Your partner tries to control your finances or limit your access to money.

❖   Your partner uses drugs or alcohol as a way to control or manipulate you.

❖   Your partner tries to isolate you from friends and family.

❖   Your partner is physically violent or threatens violence.

If any of these warning signs sound familiar to you, it's important to seek help. Whether that means talking to a therapist, reaching out to a support group, or leaving the relationship altogether, it's crucial to take steps to protect your safety and wellbeing.

In conclusion, there are clear differences between healthy and unhealthy relationships. A healthy relationship is built on mutual respect, trust, and support, while an unhealthy relationship is characterized by control, manipulation, and abuse. By learning to recognize the warning signs of an unhealthy relationship, you can take steps to protect yourself and find the love and support that you deserve.

In the words of Maya Angelou, *"The first time someone shows you who they are, believe them."* Trust your instincts and don't ignore the warning signs. You deserve to be in a healthy, loving relationship where you feel valued, respected, and safe.

Red flags in a relationship

In this chapter, I want to talk to you about red flags in relationships, based on my personal experience as a survivor of domestic abuse. These warning signs may indicate that a relationship is unhealthy or potentially abusive, and it's important to recognize them early on to protect yourself.

Jealousy and Possessiveness

One of the first red flags that I noticed in my relationship was jealousy and possessiveness. My partner would constantly ask about my whereabouts and who I was with, and would get upset if I spent time with anyone else besides them.

At first, I thought this was a sign that they cared about me, but it quickly became suffocating. It was as if they didn't trust me to make my own decisions, and they felt entitled to control my time and who I interacted with.

If your partner displays jealousy or possessiveness in a way that makes you feel uncomfortable or trapped, it may be a warning sign of an unhealthy relationship.

Controlling Behavior

Another red flag is controlling behavior. This can come in many forms, such as limiting your access to resources like money or transportation, monitoring your phone and computer usage, or dictating what you wear and how you behave.

For me, the controlling behavior was more subtle. My partner would make decisions for both of us without consulting me, or would refuse to compromise on anything. Over time, I felt like I had lost my autonomy and independence, and I was afraid to make any decisions on my own.

If your partner is constantly trying to control your behavior or decisions, it may be a sign that they are trying to exert power over you and limit your independence.

Isolation

Another warning sign is isolation. My partner would discourage me from spending time with my friends and family, and would make me feel guilty for wanting to do things on my own. They wanted me to rely solely on them for emotional support and companionship.

This isolation was damaging to my mental health, and it made it harder for me to see the warning signs of abuse. If your partner is trying to isolate you from the people and activities that bring you joy, it may be a sign of an unhealthy relationship.

Emotional Abuse

Emotional abuse is another red flag that can be harder to recognize than physical abuse. My partner would constantly put me down and make me feel like I was never good enough. They would blame me for their problems and refuse to take responsibility for their own behavior.

This emotional abuse made me feel worthless and powerless, and it took a long time for me to recognize it for what it was. If your partner is constantly belittling you or making you feel inadequate, it may be a sign of emotional abuse.

Physical and Sexual Abuse

Finally, physical and sexual abuse are obvious red flags in any relationship. No one should ever be physically or sexually assaulted by their partner. It's important to recognize the warning signs of abuse early on and seek help if you are in danger.

In conclusion, recognizing the warning signs of an unhealthy relationship is crucial to protecting yourself from abuse. Jealousy and possessiveness, controlling behavior, isolation, emotional abuse, and physical and sexual abuse are all red flags that indicate a relationship may be unhealthy or potentially abusive. Trusting your gut instincts and seeking help if you feel uncomfortable or unsafe is key to staying safe in a relationship.

Remember, abuse is never okay and you deserve to be treated with respect and dignity. If you or someone you know is experiencing any of these red flags, it's important to take action and seek support. You don't have to go through this alone.

Here are some steps you can take to protect yourself from abusive relationships:

Trust Your Instincts: If something feels off, it probably is. Don't ignore your gut instincts or try to rationalize away red flags. Trust your feelings and take action to protect yourself.

Set Boundaries: Boundaries are essential to healthy relationships. Be clear about what you will and won't tolerate in a relationship and communicate your boundaries to your partner. If they can't respect your boundaries, it may be a sign that the relationship is unhealthy.

Seek Support: Talk to a trusted friend or family member, or seek out professional help if you feel unsafe or uncomfortable in a relationship. A counselor or therapist can help you develop a safety plan and provide support as you navigate your next steps.

Practice Self-Care: Taking care of yourself is essential to staying safe in a relationship. Make time for activities you enjoy, spend time with supportive friends and family, and prioritize your physical and emotional health.

Know Your Rights: Every person has the right to live free from abuse and violence. Familiarize yourself with your legal rights and resources available to you, such as restraining orders or legal aid.

In conclusion, recognizing the warning signs of an unhealthy relationship is crucial to protecting yourself from abuse. Trust your instincts, set boundaries, seek support, practice self-care, and know your rights. Remember, you deserve to be treated with respect and dignity in all of your relationships.

Journal Exercises

Reflect on past relationships: Think about any past relationships you've had and identify any red flags you may have missed at the time. Write about how those red flags made you feel and how they may have contributed to the dynamics of the relationship.

_____

_____

_____

_____

_____

_____

_____

_____

_____

_____

_____

Identifying red flags: Make a list of potential red flags that could indicate an unhealthy relationship, such as jealousy, controlling behavior, or isolation. Then, think about whether you have experienced any of these in your current or past relationships and write about your experiences.

_____

_____

_____

_____

_____

_____

_____

_____

_____

_____

_____

_____

_____

Setting boundaries: Think about how you can set boundaries in a relationship to protect yourself from red flags. Write about what boundaries you feel comfortable setting and how you can communicate them effectively.

_____

_____

_____

_____

_____

_____

_____

_____

_____

_____

Recognizing patterns: Look for patterns in your relationships, both past and present. Do you tend to attract partners who exhibit certain red flags?

_____

_____

_____

_____

_____

_____

_____

_____

_____

_____

_____

_____

_____

Write about any patterns you've noticed and think about how you can break the cycle.

_____

_____

_____

_____

_____

_____

_____

_____

_____

_____

_____

Seeking support: If you're currently in a relationship that has red flags, consider seeking support from a therapist or a support group. Write about your thoughts and feelings around seeking help and what steps you can take to get the support you need.

_____

_____

_____

_____

_____

_____

_____

_____

_____

_____

_____

_____

_____

_____

Moving forward: Reflect on what you've learned about red flags in relationships and what steps you can take to create healthier relationships in the future. Write about any changes you plan to make and how you can stay mindful of red flags in future relationships.

_____

_____

_____

_____

_____

_____

_____

_____

_____

_____

_____

_____

_____

CHAPTER 4 ESCAPING COERCIVE CONTROL

- ❖ Planning to leave
- ❖ Safety considerations and precautions
- ❖ Support systems
- ❖ Legal options and resources

Chapter 4 focuses on the process of escaping coercive control. Leaving an abusive relationship can be a difficult and dangerous process, but it's important to remember that you are not alone and that there are resources available to help you.

This chapter will provide information on how to plan for leaving, including safety considerations and precautions that should be taken. It will also discuss the importance of support systems and the resources that are available to survivors. Additionally, we'll cover legal options for those who want to take legal action against their abuser.

It's important to remember that leaving an abusive relationship is a personal decision and that there is no right or wrong way to do it. However, by being informed and prepared, you can increase your chances of a safe and successful escape.

Planning to leave

Making the decision to leave an abusive relationship is never easy. It takes courage, strength, and a lot of planning. As a survivor of coercive control, I know firsthand how difficult it can be to leave an abusive partner. But I also know that it's possible. With the right support, resources, and safety precautions, you can take the first steps towards freedom and a brighter future.

One of the most important things you can do when planning to leave is to develop a safety plan. A safety plan is a personalized plan that outlines the steps you will take to protect yourself and your children (if you have them) from harm. Your safety plan should include a list of safe places you can go, important phone numbers, and emergency contacts. It's also a good idea to have a bag packed with essential items, such as identification documents, cash, and medication, in case you need to leave in a hurry.

It's important to remember that leaving an abusive partner can be dangerous, and you should take precautions to protect yourself. One of the first steps you can take is to change your phone number and your email address. This will help to limit your abuser's ability to contact you and to track your movements. You should also consider changing your locks, installing a security system, and notifying your workplace or school about your situation.

When it comes to leaving an abusive partner, having a strong support system is essential. This can include friends, family members, or a domestic violence hotline. You may also want to consider joining a support group for survivors of domestic violence. Being able to talk to others who have been through similar experiences can be incredibly helpful.

It's also important to consider your legal options when planning to leave an abusive partner. Depending on the circumstances of your situation, you may be able to obtain a restraining order, file for divorce or custody, or seek other legal protections. It's a good idea to consult with an attorney who specializes in domestic violence cases to understand your options.

Finally, it's important to take care of yourself during this time. Leaving an abusive relationship can be emotionally and physically exhausting. It's important to prioritize your mental and physical health, and to seek out resources that can help you heal and move forward.

This can include therapy, support groups, or self-care practices such as exercise or meditation.

In conclusion, planning to leave an abusive relationship is a difficult but necessary step towards freedom and safety. By developing a safety plan, taking precautions, building a support system, exploring legal options, and prioritizing self-care, you can take the first steps towards a brighter future. Remember, you are not alone, and there is help available.

Here's a checklist for planning to leave a coercive control relationship:

✓ Safety first: Create a safety plan for leaving and make sure to consider potential risks and dangers.

✓ Financial independence: Secure your financial independence by opening a separate bank account, establishing credit in your own name, and gathering important documents.

✓ Identify support systems: Build a network of supportive friends, family, or community resources to help you through the process.

✓ Get informed: Research your legal options and resources, such as obtaining a restraining order or seeking legal advice.

✓ Build self-care habits: Prioritize self-care by engaging in activities that bring you joy, finding a therapist or support group, and practicing self-compassion.

✓ Create an exit strategy: Develop a clear plan for leaving, including a timeline and steps to take, such as packing a bag with essentials and identifying a safe place to go.

✓ Keep a record: Document incidents of abuse, including dates, times, and details, as evidence for legal purposes.

✓ Trust your intuition: Remember that only you know what is best for yourself and trust your instincts when making decisions.

This checklist is not exhaustive and it's important to tailor it to your specific situation and needs. Remember, planning to leave a coercive control relationship can be a difficult and dangerous process, but there is support available to help you through it.

Reflect on the checklist provided for planning to leave an abusive relationship. Which steps do you feel are most important for your situation? Which steps do you feel may be the most challenging?

Think about a time when you felt scared or unsure about leaving a relationship. What thoughts or beliefs held you back from taking action? What support systems did you have in place or could have had in place to help you through the process?

Write a letter to your future self, imagining that you have successfully left an abusive relationship. What advice would you give to your present self? What words of encouragement or support would you offer?

Research and identify local resources in your community that offer support to survivors of domestic violence. Make a list of the resources available, including hotlines, counseling services, and shelters. Consider reaching out to one of these resources for support or information.

"You have within you right now, everything you need to deal with whatever the world can throw at you." - Brian Tracy

Safety considerations and precautions

It is crucial to prioritize your safety when planning to leave a coercive control situation. Leaving an abusive partner can be dangerous, and it is essential to have a safety plan in place. In this chapter, I will share my own experiences and insights on safety considerations and precautions to take when leaving a coercive control situation.

First and foremost, trust your instincts. If you feel that you are in immediate danger, call emergency services right away. If you need to leave quickly, consider keeping a packed bag in a safe location, such as at a trusted friend or family member's house or in a storage locker. Include essential items such as identification, money, and any medication you need.

It is also essential to plan a safe exit strategy. Think about the safest way to leave the situation. This might include waiting until your abuser is not home or having someone there to help you leave. Consider having a code word or signal that you can use with your support system to indicate that you need help or are in danger.

Another important consideration is to change your routine. If possible, vary your routine to make it harder for your abuser to track you down. Avoid places where you used to go together, and make sure to block them from your social media and any other means of communication.

It is also important to be mindful of technology. Your abuser may have access to your phone, computer, or other devices. Be sure to change your passwords and log out of any accounts that your abuser might have access to. Consider getting a new phone or using a friend's phone to make important calls.

Seeking support is crucial during this time. Reach out to a trusted friend or family member who can provide emotional support and help you make a plan. You can also contact a domestic violence hotline for assistance and resources. A counselor or therapist can help you process your emotions and provide you with coping strategies.

Finally, consider obtaining a restraining order or protective order. This legal document can prohibit your abuser from contacting you or coming near you. It can also provide you with legal recourse if your abuser violates the order.

In conclusion, safety considerations and precautions are essential when planning to leave a coercive control situation. Trust your instincts, plan a safe exit strategy, change your routine, be mindful of technology, seek support, and consider obtaining a restraining order. Remember, your safety is the most important consideration when leaving an abusive partner.

Journal exercises:

What safety considerations and precautions do you think would be most important for you to take when planning to leave a coercive control situation?

_____

_____

_____

_____

_____

_____

_____

_____

_____

_____

_____

_____

What support systems do you have in place, and how can you reach out to them for assistance and resources?

_____

_____

_____

_____

_____

_____

_____

_____

_____

_____

Write a letter to yourself, reminding yourself of your worth and strength as you plan to leave the abusive situation.

_____

_____

_____

_____

_____

_____

_____

_____

_____

_____

"The greatest weapon against stress is our ability to choose one thought over another." - William James

Support systems

Support systems can play a vital role in helping survivors of coercive control leave an abusive relationship and rebuild their lives. While it may be difficult to reach out for help, it is important to remember that you do not have to face this alone. There are people and resources available to support you every step of the way.

The first step in building a support system is to identify the people in your life who you can trust and rely on. This may include family members, friends, coworkers, or religious leaders. It is important to remember that not everyone in your life may be able to provide the support you need, and that is okay. Focus on the people who have shown you empathy and understanding in the past, and who you feel comfortable talking to about your situation.

It can also be helpful to seek out support from professionals who are trained in working with survivors of domestic abuse. This may include therapists, social workers, or advocates at a local domestic violence agency. These professionals can provide emotional support, help you develop a safety plan, and connect you with resources in your community.

Another important resource for survivors is support groups. Being able to connect with other people who have experienced similar situations can be incredibly validating and empowering. Support groups can also provide practical advice and strategies for coping with the challenges of leaving an abusive relationship and moving forward.

In addition to people, there are also a variety of resources available online and in your community that can provide information and support. For example, the National Domestic Violence Hotline provides confidential support and resources 24/7 at 1-800-799-SAFE (7233). Local domestic violence agencies can also provide a range of services, including emergency shelter, legal advocacy, and counseling.

When reaching out for support, it is important to keep your safety in mind. If you are still living with your abuser, consider using a safe phone or computer to reach out for help. If you are concerned about your safety, talk to your support system about developing a safety plan that can help you stay safe while leaving the relationship.

Remember, building a support system takes time and effort, but it is worth it. Having people in your corner can make all the difference as you navigate the process of leaving an abusive relationship and rebuilding your life.

In conclusion, support systems are an essential part of the healing process for survivors of coercive control. Whether it is friends and family, professionals, support groups, or resources in your community, there are people and organizations that can provide the support you need. Remember, you are not alone, and there is hope for a brighter future.

"In the midst of winter, I found there was within me an invincible summer." - Albert Camus

Legal options and resources

Legal Options and Resources: Navigating the Legal System to Escape Coercive Control

Leaving an abusive relationship can be a daunting task, but it is important to remember that you are not alone. There are legal options and resources available to help you navigate the process and ensure your safety. In this chapter, we will explore the various legal options and resources that can aid you in escaping coercive control.

The first step in navigating the legal system is to educate yourself on your rights and options. This can include consulting with a lawyer, a domestic violence advocate, or a legal aid organization. They can provide you with information on restraining orders, divorce, custody, and other legal remedies available to you.

One of the most important legal options for survivors of coercive control is obtaining a restraining order, also known as a protection order or order of protection. A restraining order is a legal document that prohibits an abuser from contacting or coming near the survivor, their children, or their home, workplace, or school. It can also grant temporary custody of children, financial support, and other forms of relief.

To obtain a restraining order, you will need to file a petition with the court. The petition will outline the abuse you have experienced and the specific protection you are seeking. A judge will review your petition and, if they find sufficient evidence of abuse, they will issue a temporary restraining order. A hearing will then be scheduled to determine whether a permanent restraining order should be granted.

It is important to note that a restraining order is not a guarantee of safety. An abuser may still attempt to violate the order, and survivors should always remain vigilant and take additional safety precautions.

Another legal option available to survivors of coercive control is divorce. Divorce is a legal process that terminates a marriage and can provide survivors with legal protections and rights. It can include division of property, child custody and support, and spousal support. Survivors should consult with a lawyer or legal aid organization to understand their options and rights when it comes to divorce.

Child custody is often a significant concern for survivors of coercive control. Courts will prioritize the safety and well-being of the child when making custody decisions, and will consider factors such as the abuser's history of abuse and the child's relationship with each parent. Survivors should document any instances of abuse or neglect by the abuser and present this evidence to the court.

Finally, survivors of coercive control can seek out additional legal resources and support. Legal aid organizations provide free or low-cost legal services to those who cannot afford a private attorney. Domestic violence advocates can provide emotional support, safety planning, and referrals to legal resources. Survivors should also consider joining a support group, where they can connect with others who have experienced similar situations.

In conclusion, navigating the legal system can be overwhelming, but there are legal options and resources available to help survivors escape coercive control. Educating yourself on your rights and options, obtaining a restraining order, pursuing divorce and child custody, and seeking out legal resources and support can all aid in the process of leaving an abusive relationship. Remember, you are not alone, and there is help available.

"You are not weak for needing help. You are strong for surviving despite your abuser's attempts to break you." -Melanie Koulouris

Some of these options and resources include:

Restraining Orders/Protection Orders: A restraining order is a legal order issued by a court that prohibits an abuser from contacting or coming near the survivor. It can also order the abuser to stay away from the survivor's home, workplace, or children's school. Protection orders offer similar legal protections to survivors.

Family Law Attorneys: Family law attorneys can assist survivors with filing for divorce, child custody, child support, and other legal matters related to leaving an abusive relationship.

Domestic Violence Hotlines: Domestic violence hotlines can provide survivors with support, information, and referrals to local resources, including legal resources.

Legal Aid Organizations: Legal aid organizations offer free or low-cost legal services to low-income individuals, including survivors of domestic violence.

Victim Advocacy Programs: Victim advocacy programs provide support, advocacy, and information to survivors of domestic violence, including information on legal options and resources.

Law Enforcement: In cases of domestic violence, survivors can contact law enforcement for assistance, including filing police reports and obtaining protective orders.

It's important for survivors to remember that there are legal options and resources available to them if they choose to leave an abusive relationship. It's also important to seek out support from friends, family, and professionals who can help with the process.

Journal Exercises

Reflect on your support system: Who are the people in your life that you can turn to for help and support?

_____

_____

_____

_____

_____

_____

_____

_____

_____

_____

_____

How have they been there for you in the past?

_____

_____

_____

_____

_____

_____

_____

_____

_____

_____

_____

What are some ways you can strengthen these relationships?

_____
_____
_____
_____
_____
_____
_____
_____
_____
_____
_____

Identify your safety plan: What are some precautions you can take to ensure your safety if you decide to leave? Write down a list of actions you can take and resources you can use.

_____
_____
_____
_____
_____
_____
_____
_____
_____
_____
_____
_____

Consider your legal options: Research the legal options available to you if you are experiencing coercive control. Write down any questions you have and make a plan to speak to a lawyer or legal advocate.

_____

_____

_____

_____

_____

_____

_____

_____

_____

_____

_____

Reflect on your self-care: How are you taking care of yourself during this difficult time? Write down some self-care practices that work for you and commit to doing them regularly.

_____

_____

_____

_____

_____

_____

_____

_____

_____

_____

_____

_____

Write a letter to yourself: Imagine you have successfully left the relationship and are now looking back at your journey. Write a letter to yourself, congratulating yourself on your strength and resilience, and offering advice to someone who may be in a similar situation.

_____

_____

_____

_____

_____

_____

_____

_____

_____

_____

_____

_____

"Strength doesn't come from what you can do. It comes from overcoming the things you once thought you couldn't." - Rikki Rogers

CHAPTER 5 HEALING FROM COERCIVE CONTROL

❖ Coping mechanisms and strategies
❖ Trauma recovery
❖ Rebuilding self-esteem and self-worth
❖ Moving on and creating a healthy future

Recovering from the effects of coercive control can be a challenging and painful process, but it is possible. In this chapter, we will explore coping mechanisms and strategies to help you manage the trauma and rebuild your self-esteem and self-worth. Healing is a journey, and it looks different for everyone. It may involve therapy, support from loved ones, and learning new ways to take care of yourself. We will also discuss trauma recovery and the importance of moving on to create a healthy future for yourself. Remember that you deserve to heal and thrive, and there is hope for a brighter tomorrow.

Coping mechanisms and strategies

Surviving and healing from coercive control can be a long and difficult journey, but there are many coping mechanisms and strategies that can help you navigate the process. While everyone's experience is different, there are a few strategies that have proven effective for many survivors. In this chapter, we'll explore some of the most effective coping mechanisms and strategies for healing from coercive control.

First, it's important to remember that self-care is crucial during this time. Taking care of yourself can be difficult when you're still dealing with the aftermath of abuse, but it's important to prioritize your physical, emotional, and mental well-being. This can include things like exercise, healthy eating, getting enough sleep, and engaging in activities that bring you joy and relaxation.

Many survivors also find it helpful to talk to a therapist or counselor. A trained mental health professional can help you work through the trauma you've experienced, develop coping mechanisms for dealing with triggers and flashbacks, and help you process any emotions that may arise as you begin to heal. Support groups for survivors of domestic violence and coercive control can also be a helpful resource, as they provide a safe and supportive space to connect with others who have had similar experiences.

Another coping mechanism that can be effective is mindfulness and meditation. This involves practicing being present in the moment, without judgment or distraction. Mindfulness can help you develop a greater sense of awareness of your emotions and thought patterns, which can help you better manage stress and anxiety.

Creative expression can also be a powerful tool for healing. Whether it's through writing, art, music, or dance, engaging in creative expression can help you process your emotions and experiences, as well as provide a positive outlet for any negative feelings you may be experiencing.

Finally, setting boundaries and saying no to things that make you uncomfortable or trigger negative emotions can be a powerful act of self-care. Learning to say no and assert your boundaries can be difficult, especially if you've been conditioned to prioritize the needs and desires of others over your own. However, setting and enforcing healthy boundaries can help you feel more in control of your life and reduce feelings of anxiety and stress.

Remember, healing from coercive control is a process, and there is no "right" way to do it. It's important to be patient and kind to yourself, and to seek out the support and resources you need to move forward.

In the next section, we'll explore trauma recovery and the specific challenges that survivors of coercive control may face in the healing process.

Write down a list of self-care activities that make you feel good. This can be anything from taking a relaxing bath to going for a walk in nature. Try to do at least one of these activities each day and reflect on how it makes you feel.

Think about a situation that triggers negative emotions for you. Write down how you usually react to this situation and how it makes you feel. Then, brainstorm alternative ways to react that may be more helpful or productive.

Write a letter to yourself, offering words of encouragement and support. Write down positive affirmations that you can read to yourself when you need a boost of confidence or reassurance.

Make a gratitude list. Write down at least five things you are grateful for each day, no matter how big or small they may be. Reflect on how these things make your life better.

Identify a specific area of your life that you want to improve. Write down small, achievable goals that will help you make progress towards that improvement. Celebrate each small success along the way.

"It is okay to be scared, but you must never let fear stop you from living your life." - Unknown

Trauma recovery

Trauma recovery is a challenging and often overwhelming journey. Survivors of coercive control may experience a wide range of emotions, including anxiety, depression, anger, and shame. It is important to understand that healing from trauma is a process, and there are steps that survivors can take to cope with and overcome their traumatic experiences.

One of the first steps in trauma recovery is acknowledging and processing the trauma. This can involve talking about the experiences with a therapist or trusted friend or family member, and allowing oneself to feel and express the emotions that come with the trauma. It is important to find a safe and supportive environment in which to do this.

Another important aspect of trauma recovery is developing coping strategies. These strategies can help survivors manage symptoms of trauma, such as flashbacks, nightmares, and anxiety. Coping strategies may include deep breathing exercises, meditation, journaling, and physical exercise. It is important to experiment with different strategies to find what works best for each individual.

Therapy can also be a valuable tool in trauma recovery. A therapist can provide a safe and non-judgmental space for survivors to process their trauma and develop coping skills. Therapy may include cognitive-behavioral therapy, which focuses on changing negative thought patterns and behaviors, or eye movement desensitization and reprocessing (EMDR), which uses rapid eye movements to help process traumatic memories.

Self-care is another important aspect of trauma recovery. This can include engaging in activities that bring joy and relaxation, such as hobbies, spending time in nature, or practicing self-compassion. It is also important to take care of physical health by getting enough sleep, eating well, and engaging in regular exercise.

Finally, it is important for survivors to recognize that healing from trauma is a journey that takes time and patience. It is common to experience setbacks or feel discouraged, but it is important to continue to prioritize self-care and seek support from loved ones or a therapist.

With time and effort, survivors can move towards a place of healing and reclaim their sense of self-worth and empowerment.

In conclusion, trauma recovery is a complex process that requires time, effort, and support. Survivors of coercive control can take steps to acknowledge and process their trauma, develop coping strategies, seek therapy, practice self-care, and recognize that healing is a journey that takes time and patience. With these tools and resources, survivors can move towards a place of healing and create a brighter future for themselves.

"In the midst of winter, I found there was, within me, an invincible summer. And that makes me happy. For it says that no matter how hard the world pushes against me, within me, there's something stronger - something better, pushing right back." - Albert Camus

Reflect on your experience of trauma. What were the initial thoughts and feelings you experienced? How have they evolved over time? Write about your journey of coping with trauma.

Describe any coping mechanisms you have used in the past to deal with your trauma. Were they helpful or harmful? How did they impact your healing process? Are there any new coping mechanisms you would like to try?

Think about the people or resources that have been helpful to you in your healing journey. Write about how they have supported you and how their presence has helped you cope with the trauma.

Write about any self-care practices you have incorporated into your life to help you manage the effects of trauma. How do these practices help you feel grounded and centered? Are there any new self-care practices you would like to explore?

Reflect on any progress you have made in your healing journey. What positive changes have you noticed in yourself? How has your perspective shifted? Write about any insights you have gained about yourself and your ability to heal from trauma.

"Healing may not be easy, but it's worth it. You deserve to live a life free from the pain of your past." - Unknown

Rebuilding self-esteem and self-worth

Rebuilding self-esteem and self-worth after experiencing coercive control can be a challenging process. It's common for survivors to feel a sense of shame, guilt, and worthlessness after being in an abusive relationship. The abuser may have repeatedly undermined your sense of self, making you question your abilities and value as a person. However, it's important to remember that you are not defined by your past experiences, and you can rebuild your sense of self-worth and self-esteem. In this chapter, we'll discuss strategies and tips for rebuilding self-esteem and self-worth.

Identify your strengths and values

One of the first steps to rebuilding your self-esteem is identifying your strengths and values. It's easy to lose sight of your positive qualities when you've been repeatedly told that you're worthless. Take some time to reflect on your values and what's important to you. Think about your strengths and what you've accomplished in the past. Write down a list of these things and refer back to it whenever you're feeling down about yourself.

Practice self-care

Self-care is an important part of rebuilding self-esteem and self-worth. Make time for activities that make you feel good, whether it's taking a warm bath, reading a book, or going for a walk in nature. Engage in activities that bring you joy and make you feel alive. Remember that taking care of yourself is not selfish; it's necessary for your well-being.

Challenge negative self-talk

Negative self-talk can be one of the biggest barriers to rebuilding self-esteem. You may find yourself believing negative thoughts such as "I'm not good enough" or "I don't deserve happiness." These thoughts are not true, and they're not helpful. Practice challenging negative self-talk by reframing negative thoughts into positive ones. For example, instead of saying "I'm not good enough," say "I am capable and deserving of love and happiness."

Surround yourself with positive people

The people you surround yourself with can have a big impact on your self-esteem. Surround yourself with people who support and encourage you. Spend time with friends and family members who make you feel good about yourself. Joining a support group or therapy group can also be helpful in providing a supportive community.

Set small achievable goals

Setting small, achievable goals can be a great way to build self-esteem. Start with small goals that are easy to achieve, such as making your bed every morning or going for a walk. As you accomplish these goals, you'll start to feel more confident and capable. Gradually increase the difficulty of your goals as you become more comfortable.

Practice self-compassion

Be kind to yourself as you go through the process of rebuilding your self-esteem. Practice self-compassion by treating yourself with the same kindness and care that you would give to a close friend. Acknowledge that healing is a process, and it takes time. Be patient and gentle with yourself.

In conclusion, rebuilding self-esteem and self-worth after experiencing coercive control can be a challenging process, but it's possible. Identify your strengths and values, practice self-care, challenge negative self-talk, surround yourself with positive people, set small achievable goals, and practice self-compassion. Remember that healing is a journey, and it takes time, but with persistence and dedication, you can regain your sense of self-worth and self-esteem.

In the words of Marianne Williamson, *"Our deepest fear is not that we are inadequate. Our deepest fear is that we are powerful beyond measure. It is our light, not our darkness that most frightens us. We ask ourselves, 'Who am I to be brilliant, gorgeous, talented, fabulous?' Actually, who are you not to be? You are a child of God."*

Journal Exercises

Reflect on past accomplishments: Take some time to reflect on past accomplishments, no matter how big or small they may seem. Write down a list of things you are proud of achieving, and how each accomplishment made you feel. Use this list to remind yourself of your strengths and abilities when you are feeling down.

_____

_____

_____

_____

_____

_____

_____

_____

_____

_____

_____

_____

Identify negative self-talk: Negative self-talk can be damaging to self-esteem and self-worth. Start paying attention to your inner dialogue and write down any negative thoughts or beliefs you have about yourself. Then, challenge these negative beliefs by questioning their validity and replacing them with positive affirmations.

_____

_____

_____

_____

_____

_____

_____

_____

_____

_____

_____

_____

_____

Practice self-care: Self-care is an important aspect of building self-esteem and self-worth. Write down a list of self-care activities that make you feel good, such as taking a relaxing bath, going for a walk in nature, or treating yourself to a favorite meal. Make time for these activities regularly and prioritize taking care of yourself.

_____

_____

_____

_____

_____

_____

_____

_____

_____

_____

_____

_____

Identify and challenge limiting beliefs: Limiting beliefs can hold us back from reaching our full potential. Write down any limiting beliefs you have about yourself or your abilities, and then challenge these beliefs by identifying evidence that contradicts them. For example, if you believe you are not smart enough to pursue a certain career, write down instances where you have demonstrated intelligence or received positive feedback on your abilities.

_____

_____

_____

_____

_____

_____

_____

_____

_____

_____

_____

_____

Set achievable goals: Setting and achieving goals can help build self-esteem and self-worth. Write down a list of achievable goals, both short-term and long-term, and break them down into smaller, actionable steps. As you work towards achieving your goals, celebrate your progress and acknowledge your accomplishments.

_____

_____

_____

_____

_____

_____

_____

_____

_____

_____

_____

_____

_____

_____

"The moment you start valuing yourself, the world will start valuing you." - Unknown

Moving on and creating a healthy future

Moving on and creating a healthy future after experiencing coercive control can be a difficult and challenging process. However, with time and effort, it is possible to heal from the trauma and rebuild a happy and fulfilling life. In this chapter, we will explore some of the strategies and steps that survivors can take to move forward and create a healthy future.

The first step in moving on from an abusive relationship is to acknowledge and process the trauma. This involves facing the emotions and memories associated with the abuse, which can be painful and difficult. However, avoiding or denying the trauma can lead to unresolved feelings that may surface later in life.

One effective coping mechanism for trauma recovery is therapy. Seeking professional help from a therapist or counselor can provide survivors with a safe space to process their trauma and work through the emotions associated with it. Therapy can also provide survivors with practical coping strategies and tools to help them manage anxiety, depression, and other mental health issues that may arise as a result of the trauma.

Another important aspect of moving on is establishing healthy boundaries. Survivors may have learned to tolerate abuse or have had their boundaries violated repeatedly during the abusive relationship. Setting and enforcing healthy boundaries is essential to establishing a sense of safety and control over one's life. This can involve learning to say "no" to situations or people that do not feel safe or comfortable, and practicing assertive communication.

In addition to therapy and boundary-setting, self-care is crucial in the healing process. This can involve engaging in activities that bring joy and relaxation, such as exercise, meditation, or creative pursuits. Eating a healthy and balanced diet, getting enough sleep, and practicing good hygiene can also promote physical and emotional well-being.

Building a support system is another essential component of moving on from coercive control. Survivors may have been isolated or cut off from friends and family during the abusive relationship, so it is important to reconnect with loved ones and build new relationships. Joining support groups or online communities of other survivors can also provide a sense of connection and validation.

Finally, it is important for survivors to focus on creating a positive and fulfilling future. This can involve setting goals and working towards achieving them, whether it is returning to school, pursuing a new career, or engaging in volunteer work. It may also involve exploring new hobbies or interests and rediscovering the things that bring joy and fulfillment.

In conclusion, moving on from coercive control is a challenging but essential process for survivors. Acknowledging and processing the trauma, seeking professional help, setting healthy boundaries, engaging in self-care, building a support system, and focusing on creating a positive future are all important steps in this journey. With time, effort, and support, survivors can heal and rebuild a happy and fulfilling life.

I hope this chapter has been helpful in providing guidance and support to survivors of coercive control. Remember, healing is possible, and you are not alone in your journey.

"You are not what happened to you, you are what you choose to become." - Carl Jung

Journal Exercises

Reflect on your values and priorities: What are the most important things to you in life?

_____

_____

_____

_____

_____

_____

_____

_____

_____

_____

_____

_____

What values do you hold dear? Take some time to write down your top values and priorities. Once you have a clear understanding of what matters most to you, it will be easier to make decisions that align with your values and create a fulfilling future.

_____

_____

_____

_____

_____

_____

_____

_____

_____

_____

_____

_____

Identify your goals: What do you want to achieve in the future?

_____

_____

_____

_____

_____

_____

_____

_____

_____

_____

What steps can you take to make those goals a reality?

_____

_____

_____

_____

_____

_____

_____

_____

_____

_____

_____

_____

Write down your goals and break them down into smaller, more manageable steps. Celebrate your progress along the way and don't be afraid to adjust your goals as needed.

_____

_____

_____

_____

_____

_____

_____

_____

_____

_____

_____

Practice gratitude: Even in the midst of difficult times, there are always things to be grateful for. Take time each day to write down a few things you are thankful for. Focusing on the positive can help shift your mindset and increase your overall sense of well-being.

_____
_____
_____
_____
_____
_____
_____
_____
_____
_____
_____

Cultivate healthy relationships: Surround yourself with people who support and uplift you. Make an effort to cultivate healthy relationships with friends, family, and other supportive individuals. Seek out opportunities to connect with others who share your interests and values.

_____
_____
_____
_____
_____
_____

_____

_____

_____

_____

_____

_____

Engage in self-care: Make time for activities that nourish your mind, body, and spirit. This might include things like exercise, meditation, journaling, or spending time in nature. Prioritizing self-care can help you feel more balanced and resilient as you move forward.

_____

_____

_____

_____

_____

_____

_____

_____

_____

_____

_____

_____

_____

"The only way to make sense out of change is to plunge into it, move with it, and join the dance." - Alan Watts

CHAPTER 6 RISING STRONG AFTER COERCIVE CONTROL

- ❖ Redefining self and values
- ❖ Establishing healthy boundaries and relationships
- ❖ Advocacy and activism
- ❖ Living a life of freedom and fulfillment

The journey of healing and recovery from coercive control is not an easy one, but it is possible. As survivors begin to rebuild their lives and reclaim their sense of self, they may find themselves redefining their values and priorities. This process involves taking a step back and reflecting on what truly matters to them, and redefining what success and happiness mean on their own terms.

Part of this process involves establishing healthy boundaries and relationships, which may require learning new communication skills and identifying toxic patterns of behavior. Survivors may also find themselves drawn to advocacy and activism, using their experiences to educate others and promote change in society.

Ultimately, the goal is to live a life of freedom and fulfillment, one that is not defined by past trauma but by a sense of purpose and passion. In this chapter, we will explore how survivors can rise strong after coercive control and create a life that is full of joy, meaning, and fulfillment.

Redefining self and values

Redefining self and values after experiencing coercive control is a crucial step in the healing process. Survivors often find themselves feeling lost, confused, and disconnected from their sense of self, as they were conditioned to prioritize their abuser's needs and desires over their own. However, it's important to remember that it's never too late to rediscover who you are and what you stand for.

One way to begin this process is by engaging in self-reflection and introspection. Take some time to sit with yourself and think about what matters most to you. What are your passions, values, and beliefs? What brings you joy and fulfillment? What are some things that you want to achieve in your life?

It's important to also acknowledge and address any negative self-talk or limiting beliefs that you may be holding onto as a result of the abuse. These beliefs may include feelings of worthlessness, shame, or inadequacy. Challenge these beliefs by focusing on your strengths and accomplishments, and by reminding yourself of your inherent value and worth as a human being.

In addition to self-reflection, seeking out therapy or support groups can also be helpful in the process of redefining self and values. A therapist or support group can provide a safe and non-judgmental space to explore and process your thoughts and feelings, and can offer guidance and support as you navigate this journey.

Remember, rediscovering and redefining yourself is a journey, and it's okay to take your time. Be patient and compassionate with yourself, and trust that with time and effort, you can create a fulfilling and meaningful life that aligns with your true self and values.

Journal Exercises

What are the values that are most important to you?

_____

_____

_____

_____

_____

_____

_____

_____

_____

_____

_____

_____

Are they different from the values you had before experiencing coercive control? How have they changed?

_____

_____

_____

_____

_____

_____

_____

_____

_____

_____

_____

_____

Think about a time when you felt like you weren't being true to yourself. How did that make you feel?

_____

_____

_____

_____

_____

_____

_____

_____

_____

_____

_____

_____

What can you do to ensure you stay true to yourself and your values in the future?

_____

_____

_____

_____

_____

_____

_____

_____

_____

_____

_____

What are some things that you used to enjoy doing before the relationship turned unhealthy?

_____

_____

_____

_____

_____

_____

_____

_____

_____

_____

_____

_____

Is there anything stopping you from doing those things now?

_____

_____

_____

_____

_____

_____

_____

_____

What steps can you take to start doing those things again?

_____

_____

_____

_____

_____

_____

_____

_____

_____

_____

_____

_____

Write down three positive affirmations that reflect your new sense of self and values. Repeat these affirmations to yourself every day for a week.

_____

_____

_____

_____

_____

_____

_____

_____

_____

_____

Reflect on a time when you were proud of yourself for standing up for your values or beliefs. What did you learn from that experience?

_____

_____

_____

_____

_____

_____

_____

_____

_____

_____

_____

_____

Write a letter to your younger self, sharing the values and insights you've gained from your experiences with coercive control. What advice would you give yourself?

_____

_____

_____

_____

_____

_____

_____

_____

_____

_____

How would you encourage yourself to stay strong and true to your values?

_____

_____

_____

_____

_____

_____

_____

_____

_____

_____

_____

_____

_____

What are some new experiences or challenges that you're excited
to pursue now that you're free from the confines of an unhealthy
relationship? Make a list of these things and set some goals for yourself
to achieve them.

_____

_____

_____

_____

_____

_____

_____

_____

_____

_____

_____

Reflect on the progress you've made in redefining yourself and
your values since leaving the abusive relationship. What steps have you
taken to grow and change?

_____

_____

_____

_____

_____

_____

_____

_____

_____

_____

_____

What still needs work?

_____

_____

_____

_____

_____

_____

_____

_____

_____

_____

What is your plan for continuing to grow and evolve in the future?

_____

_____

_____

_____

_____

_____

_____

_____

_____

_____

_____

_____

_____

_____

"You yourself, as much as anybody in the entire universe, deserve your love and affection." - Buddha

Establishing healthy boundaries and relationships

Establishing healthy boundaries and relationships is an essential part of recovering from coercive control. When someone has experienced years of abuse and manipulation, it can be challenging to know what healthy relationships look like or how to set healthy boundaries. However, with some guidance and practice, it is possible to create a life filled with healthy relationships and positive experiences.

The first step in establishing healthy boundaries and relationships is to recognize that you are worthy of respect and love. After experiencing abuse, it's common to feel like you don't deserve these things, but this couldn't be further from the truth. Everyone deserves to be treated with respect, kindness, and compassion, regardless of their past experiences.

Once you've internalized the fact that you deserve healthy relationships, the next step is to set boundaries. Boundaries are personal guidelines that help you define what is and isn't acceptable in your relationships. They can help you protect your physical and emotional well-being and create a sense of safety and security.

There are several different types of boundaries that you may need to set, depending on your situation. Some common examples include:

Physical boundaries: These boundaries involve physical touch and personal space. For example, you may need to set boundaries around hugging, kissing, or other types of physical contact.

Emotional boundaries: Emotional boundaries involve setting limits around your thoughts and feelings. For example, you may need to set boundaries around what topics you're willing to discuss or how much emotional support you're comfortable providing to others.

Time boundaries: Time boundaries involve setting limits around your schedule and how you spend your time. For example, you may need to set boundaries around how much time you spend with certain people or how often you take on extra responsibilities.

Material boundaries: Material boundaries involve setting limits around your possessions and finances. For example, you may need to set boundaries around sharing money or lending out your belongings.

Setting boundaries can be challenging, especially if you've never done it before. It's important to remember that it's okay to start small and work your way up. You don't have to set every boundary all at once. Instead, try starting with one or two boundaries that feel manageable and work your way up from there.

It's also important to communicate your boundaries clearly and assertively. This can be difficult if you're used to people not respecting your boundaries, but it's essential if you want to create healthy relationships. Be clear and direct about what you need and how others can respect your boundaries.

Another key part of establishing healthy relationships is learning to trust yourself and your instincts. After experiencing abuse, it's common to feel like you can't trust your own judgment. However, learning to trust yourself is a crucial part of creating healthy relationships. Practice listening to your instincts and taking action when something feels off.

Finally, it's important to surround yourself with supportive people who respect your boundaries and help you feel safe and valued. This may include friends, family members, or a support group of other survivors. Building a network of supportive people can help you feel less alone and more empowered as you move forward.

In conclusion, establishing healthy boundaries and relationships is an essential part of recovering from coercive control. It takes time, practice, and patience, but with the right tools and support, it's possible to create a life filled with healthy relationships, respect, and love. Remember, you deserve to be treated with kindness and compassion, and it's never too late to start creating the life you deserve.

Journal Exercises

Reflect on your past relationships, both romantic and platonic. Were there any instances where you felt like your boundaries were crossed or that the relationship was unhealthy?

_____

_____

_____

_____

_____

_____

_____

_____

_____

_____

_____

_____

_____

What were some of the warning signs you noticed?

_____

_____

_____

_____

_____

_____

_____

_____

_____

_____

How can you use this knowledge to establish healthier boundaries in your current relationships?

_____

_____

_____

_____

_____

_____

_____

_____

_____

_____

_____

_____

_____

Think about what boundaries are most important to you in a
relationship. These can be physical boundaries, emotional boundaries,
or even social boundaries. Write down why each boundary is important
to you and what you would do if someone were to cross that boundary.

_____

_____

_____

_____

_____

_____

_____

_____

_____

_____

_____

Consider the people in your life right now. Are there any
relationships that are causing you stress or discomfort?

_____

_____

_____

_____

_____

_____

_____

_____

_____

_____

_____

_____

_____

Are there any relationships where you feel like your boundaries are being ignored or disregarded?

_____

_____

_____

_____

_____

_____

_____

_____

_____

_____

Write about how you can communicate your boundaries to these people in a clear and assertive way.

_____

_____

_____

_____

_____

_____

_____

_____

_____

_____

_____

_____

_____

Take some time to reflect on your own needs and values. What do you need in a relationship in order to feel fulfilled and happy?

_____

_____

_____

_____

_____

_____

_____

_____

_____

_____

What are your deal breakers? Write about how you can communicate these needs and values to potential partners or friends.

Think about your communication style. Are you someone who tends to avoid conflict or confrontation?

_____

_____

_____

_____

_____

_____

_____

_____

_____

_____

_____

Or are you someone who is quick to anger?

_____

_____

_____

_____

_____

_____

_____

_____

Write about how you can practice assertive communication in
order to establish and maintain healthy boundaries in your relationships.

_____

_____

_____
_____
_____
_____
_____
_____
_____
_____
_____
_____
_____

"Boundaries are a part of self-care. They are healthy, normal, and necessary." - Doreen Virtue

Advocacy and activism

Advocacy and activism are powerful tools for survivors of coercive control. They allow us to not only heal from our own experiences but also to make a positive impact on the lives of others who may be experiencing similar situations. Advocacy involves using our own experiences to educate and raise awareness about the issue of coercive control, while activism involves taking action to bring about change at a larger level.

As survivors, we have a unique perspective and understanding of the complexities and impact of coercive control. Our stories can be powerful tools for raising awareness and educating others about the signs and effects of this form of abuse. By sharing our experiences with others, we can help to break the silence and stigma surrounding coercive control and encourage more people to speak out and seek help.

One way to advocate for change is to get involved with organizations or groups that focus on domestic violence and coercive control. These groups often provide support for survivors, as well as resources for education and advocacy. They may also provide opportunities to get involved in activism efforts, such as advocating for policy changes or participating in awareness-raising campaigns.

Another way to advocate is to share your story through various channels, such as social media, writing, or public speaking. You can also reach out to local community organizations, schools, or businesses to share your story and provide education about the signs of coercive control. By raising awareness and educating others, we can help to prevent others from experiencing the same trauma we did.

In addition to advocacy, survivors can also get involved in activism efforts to bring about change at a larger level. This may involve joining protests or rallies, contacting elected officials to advocate for policy changes, or starting your own advocacy campaign. Activism efforts can be a powerful way to bring attention to the issue of coercive control and push for systemic change that can benefit survivors and prevent future abuse.

Advocacy and activism can also be an important part of the healing process for survivors. By taking action and making a positive impact on the lives of others, survivors can reclaim a sense of agency and control over their own lives. It can be empowering to turn our pain into action and work towards creating a world where coercive control is no longer tolerated.

In conclusion, advocacy and activism are important tools for survivors of coercive control. By sharing our stories and getting involved in advocacy and activism efforts, we can raise awareness about the issue of coercive control and work towards creating a safer and more equitable world for survivors. These efforts can also be an important part of the healing process, allowing survivors to reclaim their sense of agency and create a fulfilling and meaningful life after the trauma of coercive control.

There are many resources available for survivors looking to get involved in advocacy and activism. Here are a few:

National Coalition Against Domestic Violence (NCADV) - NCADV is an organization dedicated to ending domestic violence through education, public policy, and advocacy. They offer a variety of resources and programs for survivors, as well as opportunities to get involved in advocacy efforts.

Domestic Violence Legal Empowerment and Appeals Project (DV LEAP) - DV LEAP is a nonprofit organization that provides legal representation and advocacy for survivors of domestic violence. They work to ensure that survivors have access to the legal resources they need to protect themselves and their families.

National Domestic Violence Hotline - The National Domestic Violence Hotline provides crisis counseling and referrals for survivors of domestic violence. They also offer resources for those who want to get involved in advocacy and activism.

Women's March - Women's March is a global movement dedicated to advancing women's rights and promoting social justice. They organize events and campaigns around the world to promote gender equality and support survivors of domestic violence.

RAINN (Rape, Abuse & Incest National Network) - RAINN is the largest anti-sexual violence organization in the United States. They offer a variety of resources and programs for survivors of domestic violence, as well as opportunities to get involved in advocacy and activism.

These are just a few examples of the many resources available for survivors looking to get involved in advocacy and activism. It's important to find an organization or cause that aligns with your values and goals, and to remember that even small actions can make a big difference in creating positive change.

Journal Exercises

What are some of the boundaries that I need to set for myself in my personal relationships?

_____

_____

_____

_____

_____

_____

_____

_____

_____

_____

_____

How can I communicate these boundaries to my loved ones in a healthy and respectful way?

_____

_____

_____

_____

_____

_____

_____

_____

Have there been times in the past where I have felt uncomfortable in a relationship but ignored my instincts?

How can I learn to trust my gut and establish boundaries to protect myself in the future?

_____

_____

_____

_____

_____

_____

What are some signs that a relationship may not be healthy or may be crossing my boundaries?

_____

_____

_____

_____

_____

_____

_____

_____

_____

_____

How can I recognize these warning signs and take action to protect myself?

_____

_____

_____

_____

_____

_____

_____

_____

_____

_____

_____

_____

_____

How can I practice self-care and prioritize my own needs while also maintaining healthy relationships with those around me?

_____

_____

_____

_____

_____

_____

_____

_____

_____

_____

_____

What are some ways that I can effectively communicate my boundaries and needs to others without feeling guilty or ashamed?

_____

_____

_____

_____

_____

_____

_____

_____

_____

_____

_____

_____

How can I build up my self-confidence and assertiveness in
relationships?

_____

_____

_____

_____

_____

_____

_____

_____

_____

_____

Are there any relationships in my life that are currently causing me
stress or anxiety?

_____

_____

_____

_____

_____

_____

_____

_____

_____

_____

_____

_____

How can I address these issues and work towards creating a healthier dynamic in the future?

_____

_____

_____

_____

_____

_____

_____

_____

_____

_____

What are some of the benefits of establishing healthy boundaries in relationships?

_____

_____

_____

_____

_____

_____

_____

_____

_____

_____

_____

_____

_____

How can I envision a future where I am able to maintain these boundaries and live a happier, more fulfilling life?

_____

_____

_____

_____

_____

_____

_____

_____

_____

_____

_____

Remember to approach these journal prompts with honesty and self-compassion. There is no "right" or "wrong" way to establish boundaries in relationships, and it's important to take things at your own pace and prioritize your own well-being.

Living a life of freedom and fulfillment

Living a life of freedom and fulfillment after experiencing coercive control may seem like an impossible feat, but it is possible. It takes time, patience, and a willingness to make changes and take risks. In this chapter, we will discuss ways to break free from the chains of coercive control and live a life that is fulfilling and full of joy.

One of the first steps in living a life of freedom and fulfillment is to identify what that means for you. What are your passions and interests? What brings you joy and fulfillment? Take time to explore these things and figure out what matters most to you. Coercive control can strip away a victim's sense of self and agency, so it's important to rediscover those things and start building a life around them.

It's also important to surround yourself with people who support and uplift you. This may mean cutting ties with toxic people from your past or building new relationships with people who understand and respect your boundaries. Building a strong support system can help you navigate the challenges of rebuilding your life after coercive control.

In addition to building a support system, it's important to establish healthy boundaries in all areas of your life. This means being clear about what you will and will not tolerate, and sticking to those boundaries even when it's difficult. It may mean saying no to people or situations that don't align with your values and priorities. It may also mean setting boundaries with yourself, such as prioritizing self-care and taking time to recharge.

Another important aspect of living a life of freedom and fulfillment is to focus on personal growth and development. This may mean learning new skills, pursuing education or career goals, or engaging in therapy or other forms of self-improvement. It's important to remember that healing is a lifelong journey, and there is always room for growth and improvement.

Finally, living a life of freedom and fulfillment often involves giving back to others and making a positive impact in the world. This may mean volunteering for a cause you believe in, engaging in activism or advocacy work, or simply being kind and supportive to those around you. Making a difference in the lives of others can bring a sense of purpose and fulfillment that is difficult to find elsewhere.

In conclusion, living a life of freedom and fulfillment after experiencing coercive control is possible, but it takes time and effort. It involves rediscovering your sense of self and agency, building a strong support system, establishing healthy boundaries, focusing on personal growth and development, and giving back to others. It's a journey that can be difficult, but it's also one that is incredibly rewarding and empowering.

Journal Exercises

What does freedom mean to you?

_____

_____

_____

_____

_____

_____

_____

_____

_____

_____

Reflect on the ways in which you have experienced freedom in your
life and the ways in which you still crave it.

_____

_____

_____

_____

_____

_____

_____

_____

_____

_____

Write about a time when you felt truly fulfilled. What were you doing?

_____

_____

_____

_____

_____

_____

_____

_____

_____

Who were you with? What made that moment so special?

_____

_____

_____

_____

_____

_____

_____

_____

_____

_____

Identify three goals or aspirations that you have for your life. What steps can you take to start working towards these goals?

_____

_____

_____

_____

_____

_____

_____

_____

_____

_____

What are some self-care practices that make you feel fulfilled and balanced?

_____

_____

_____

_____

_____

_____

_____

_____

_____

_____

_____

How can you incorporate more of these practices into your daily life?

_____

_____

_____

_____

_____

_____

_____

_____

_____

_____

_____

_____

_____

Reflect on your values and beliefs. How have these evolved over time?

_____

_____

_____

_____

_____

_____

_____

_____

_____

Are there any values that you hold now that conflict with those of your former abuser?

_____

_____

_____

_____

_____

_____

_____

_____

_____

_____

How can you stay true to your values as you move forward in your life?

_____

_____

_____

_____

_____

_____

_____

_____

_____

Write a letter to your future self, describing the life you want to lead and the person you want to be. What steps can you take today to start creating that future?

_____

_____

_____

_____

_____

_____

_____

_____

_____

_____

Think about the people in your life who bring you joy and support.
How can you cultivate those relationships and make them a priority?

_____

_____

_____

_____

_____

_____

_____

_____

_____

Write about a time when you faced a challenge and overcame it. What
did you learn from that experience?

_____

_____

_____

_____

_____

_____

_____

_____

_____

_____

_____

_____

_____

How can you use that knowledge to overcome future challenges?

_____

_____

_____

_____

_____

_____

_____

_____

_____

_____

_____

Reflect on the ways in which you have grown and changed since
leaving your abusive relationship. What strengths have you developed?

_____

_____

_____

_____

_____

_____

_____

_____

_____

_____

_____

How have you become more resilient?

_____

_____

_____

_____

_____

_____

_____

_____

_____

Write down three things that you are grateful for each day. This can be as simple as a beautiful sunset or a kind gesture from a friend.

_____

_____

_____

_____

_____

_____

Practicing gratitude can help you cultivate a more positive mindset and increase your overall sense of fulfillment.

CHAPTER 7 CONCLUSION

- ❖ Recap of key points
- ❖ Encouragement and hope for the future
- ❖ Resources for additional support

Throughout this book, we have explored the topic of coercive control and its devastating impact on victims. We have looked at the signs of coercive control, the dynamics of abusive relationships, the effects of abuse on the victim, and the journey of healing and recovery.

In this concluding chapter, we will recap some of the key points discussed in the book, offer encouragement and hope for the future, and provide additional resources for support.

It is important to remember that coercive control is a serious form of abuse that can have far-reaching and long-lasting effects on victims. It can affect a victim's mental and emotional well-being, their physical health, and their ability to form healthy relationships in the future.

However, it is possible to heal and recover from the trauma of coercive control. With the right support and resources, victims can learn to recognize the signs of abusive relationships, establish healthy boundaries, and build fulfilling and meaningful lives.

In the following sections, we will recap some of the key points discussed in the book and provide resources for additional support.

Recap of key points

As we near the end of this book, it is important to recap the key points that we have covered. Survivors of coercive control often struggle with identifying the abuse they have experienced, as it can be insidious and difficult to detect. Coercive control involves a pattern of behavior that is used to gain and maintain power and control over another person, often through isolation, manipulation, and intimidation.

One of the most important things for survivors to understand is that coercive control is not their fault. They did not cause the abuse, and they are not responsible for their abuser's behavior. This can be a difficult concept to accept, particularly when the abuser has been successful in gaslighting or blaming the survivor for their actions.

Recovery from coercive control can be a long and challenging process. It often involves addressing the physical and emotional effects of abuse, as well as the practical challenges of rebuilding a life after leaving an abusive relationship. However, with the right support and resources, survivors can heal and go on to lead happy, fulfilling lives.

It is also important to recognize the role that societal attitudes and systems play in perpetuating coercive control. This includes everything from victim blaming and shaming to the lack of resources and support for survivors. To truly address the issue of coercive control, we must work to change these systems and create a culture that prioritizes healthy relationships and respect for all individuals.

In conclusion, the key points to remember from this book are:

Coercive control is a pattern of behavior used to gain and maintain power and control over another person
Survivors are not responsible for their abuser's behavior and should not be blamed for the abuse they have experienced
Recovery from coercive control can be a long and challenging process, but with the right support and resources, survivors can heal and thrive
Societal attitudes and systems play a role in perpetuating coercive control, and we must work to change these systems to create a culture that prioritizes healthy relationships and respect for all individuals.
By understanding these key points and continuing to educate ourselves and others about the issue of coercive control, we can work

towards creating a world where everyone is able to live free from abuse and violence.

Encouragement and hope for the future

Of all the things that a survivor of coercive control can feel after escaping an abusive relationship, hope may be the most difficult to come by. After all, the abuser may have spent years convincing the survivor that they are worthless, that they will never be able to make it on their own, and that no one will ever love them. It can be hard to believe that a life of happiness and fulfillment is even possible after such an experience.

But the truth is that hope and healing are possible. It may take time, and it may not always be easy, but with the right support and resources, survivors of coercive control can find a path forward towards a life of freedom and fulfillment.

One of the most important things that survivors can do for themselves is to seek out the support they need to heal. This may include therapy, support groups, or other forms of counseling. Working with a professional can help survivors to process their experiences, understand the dynamics of the abusive relationship, and develop coping strategies for the future.

Another important step towards healing is to take care of oneself physically, emotionally, and spiritually. This might include getting regular exercise, eating a healthy diet, practicing relaxation techniques like meditation or yoga, and finding ways to connect with one's sense of purpose and meaning in life.

It's also important for survivors to build a strong support network of friends and loved ones who can provide encouragement, love, and practical support when needed. This may mean reaching out to old friends who were pushed away by the abuser, or building new relationships with people who understand what the survivor has been through.

Perhaps most importantly, survivors need to remember that healing is a journey, not a destination. There may be setbacks and difficult moments along the way, but each step forward is a victory. With time, patience, and the right resources, survivors can build a new life for themselves that is free from the shadow of coercive control.

It's also important for survivors to remember that they are not alone. There are countless others who have been through similar experiences, and who have found hope and healing on the other side. By sharing their stories, survivors can help to break the cycle of abuse and build a world where coercive control is no longer tolerated.

Finally, it's important to remember that the road to healing is not always linear. There may be times when old wounds are reopened or when new challenges arise. But by staying committed to the process of healing and growth, survivors can build a life that is filled with love, joy, and purpose.

In the end, the most important message for survivors of coercive control is one of hope. No matter how dark the present may seem, there is always a path forward towards a brighter future. With the right support and resources, survivors can break free from the cycle of abuse and build a life that is defined by their own values, dreams, and passions.

Resources for additional support

National Domestic Violence Hotline: Provides 24/7 support and resources for anyone experiencing domestic violence in the United States. Call 1-800-799-7233 or visit their website at www.thehotline.org.

Loveisrespect: Offers confidential support and resources for young people experiencing dating abuse in the United States. Call 1-866-331-9474 or visit their website at www.loveisrespect.org.

RAINN (Rape, Abuse & Incest National Network): Provides support and resources for survivors of sexual violence in the United States. Call 1-800-656-4673 or visit their website at www.rainn.org.

National Center for Victims of Crime: Provides resources and support for victims of all types of crime in the United States. Visit their website at www.victimsofcrime.org.

International Directory of Domestic Violence Agencies: Offers a comprehensive list of domestic violence agencies and resources by country. Visit their website at www.hotpeachpages.net.

Women's Aid: Provides support and resources for women experiencing domestic violence in the United Kingdom. Call their 24-hour helpline at 0808 2000 247 or visit their website at www.womensaid.org.uk.

The Samaritans: Offers emotional support for anyone experiencing distress or suicidal thoughts in the United Kingdom. Call their 24-hour helpline at 116 123 or visit their website at www.samaritans.org.

National Network of Women's Shelters and Centers in Brazil: Provides support and resources for survivors of domestic violence in Brazil. Visit their website at www.spm.gov.br.

Lifeline Australia: Offers support and resources for anyone experiencing a personal crisis in Australia. Call their 24-hour helpline at 13 11 14 or visit their website at www.lifeline.org.au.

National Centre for Domestic Violence: Provides support and resources for victims of domestic violence in the United Kingdom. Call their 24-hour helpline at 0800 970 2070 or visit their website at www.ncdv.org.uk.

These resources are just a starting point, and there may be many more organizations and hotlines available in your local area. It is important to reach out for support and to know that you are not alone in your journey towards healing and recovery.

www.ingramcontent.com/pod-product-compliance
Lightning Source LLC
Chambersburg PA
CBHW070721130626
46553CB00005B/2089